MONTANA

EAST OF THE MOUNTAINS

VOL. 2

TEXT AND PHOTOS BY RICK AND SUSIE GRAETZ

The Montana Series

NUMBER FOUR

PHOTOGRAPHY CONTRIBUTIONS BY:

Erwin and Peggy Bauer ▪ Douglass Dye ▪ Chuck Haney
John Lambing ▪ Harold E. Malde ▪ Larry Mayer ▪ Salvatore Vasapolli

2

The blacktailed prairie dog is essential to the survival and well being of 130 species of animals.
ERWIN AND PEGGY BAUER

From the Tripp Divide looking across to the U L Bend of the Missouri River.
RICK AND SUSIE GRAETZ

©2000 Northern Rockies Publishing
Rick and Susie Graetz
P.O. Box 1707, Helena, Montana 59624
norockpub@aol.com

Design by GingerBee Graphics

All color, design and prepress work done in Montana, U.S.A.
Printed in Korea
Softcover: ISBN 1-891152-07-6
Hardcover: ISBN 1-891152-12-2

Front Cover:
Cow Island on the Wild and Scenic Missouri.
RICK AND SUSIE GRAETZ

Back Cover:
Great falls of the Missouri at Great Falls.
RICK AND SUSIE GRAETZ

MONTANA — EAST OF THE MOUNTAINS

By Rick and Susie Graetz

The essay written for Volume I covered this province well and launched our efforts to portray the magnificent diversity and beauty of the country that stretches east of Montana's Northern Rocky Mountains to the Dakotas. Here, in our second collection of images and words, that enjoyable task continues.

This land of big waters, simple grandeur, endless vistas and an unending sky is one of America's great pieces of geography. The landscape dominates. Much of the territory hasn't changed since the days when it was the domain of the nomadic Indian nations.

History is recent and alive. The Old West of legend was played out here. Just a bit more than 100 years ago, the characters of those times...cattle barons, gold seekers, outlaws, cowboys, vigilantes, rustlers and horse thieves went about their ways in these settings. And the American cowboy still makes his living on its sprawling ranches. Signs of the era of the first sodbusters are everywhere. It remains the Real Montana!

A distinct region unto itself, Montana east of the mountains harbors unique landforms. Badlands, sculptured sandstone, river breaks, wildlife refuges, island mountain ranges, as well as smaller bits of geologic wonderment, intermingle with grand scenes. Space, much of it undisturbed, is its greatest commodity. This immense, spread out land, delivers a feeling of no borders or confinement where a human can stretch and breath...freedom prevails.

Its places of beauty, to name just a few, include stretches of the Missouri River that take in 150 miles of a Wild and Scenic corridor as well as 145 miles of the Charles M. Russell National Wildlife Refuge, the eroded and beautiful Makoshika and Terry badlands, the untamed Yellowstone River, the glacial scraped plains and

Sugar beet crop in the Yellowstone Valley near Sidney.
CHUCK HANEY

pothole lands near Plentywood, the lonesome breaks of the Powder and Tongue rivers, the Sweetgrass Hills and the stunning Rocky Mountain Front that defines the western ramparts of the region.

Out here a formidable canopy of sky provides a constantly changing panorama... a playing field for clouds and weather. From the moment the sun bursts onto the clear eastern horizon of Montana beginning its journey towards the closing of day, many surprises may appear depending upon the mood of the heavens.

Summer thunderstorms build to a towering collection of billowy white and gray clouds that are then swept by the wind up into Canada or out onto the Dakotas or Wyoming plains leaving brilliant sunshine over the prairie, often only to be replaced by another storm with intense lightning displays.

In winter, northern born blizzards roll like turbulent waves across the uncluttered skyline depositing a quiet comforter of snow in their wake.

The abundance of wildlife from elk and bighorn sheep, to the smallest of critters occupying every reach of this domain is legendary. Its waterfowl population is especially incredible. Refuges, ponds and waterways witness massive conventions every spring and fall as convoys of ducks, geese and birds come and go with the seasons. Observing their raucous presence is a spectacular encounter.

Most of all, Montana east of the mountains is one fine place to get familiar with. An added lure to the colorful past and grandeur of open spaces, is the sense of permanency folks who make their home and living in the small, well spaced towns, ranches and farms have. Many in these parts are descendants of early-day homesteaders or products of cattle outfits that have been in the same family for generations; others simply chose to live in this prairie environment. Communities are neat and peaceful, a profile dictated by the rural life that characterizes this corner of the Great Plains.

The towns are the essence of a territory where the natural features capture attention. Social and commercial activities interact within them in a way that is all but disappearing across America. Cafes, hardware and grocery stores are where stockmen, farmers, implement dealers and bankers meet to discuss ag-economics, their families, and the weather. You'll still find drug stores with soda fountains and chances are that you can walk in the door of any business and shake the hand of the owner. A genuine welcoming atmosphere prevails.

Its *places of beauty*

include the 150-mile stretch of the Wild and

Scenic Missouri River.

Cottonwoods along
the Missouri River.
RICK AND SUSIE GRAETZ

To the uninitiated, many of these eastern Montana hamlets might seem carefree, but the problems of a lagging agricultural economy, lack of opportunities for the young, and drought are real. The people of these isolated havens that dot the vast prairie deal with them and never give up. A "can do" attitude holds sway over town meetings or at the supper table as residents look for answers and new possibilities...hope always seems to be there.

They also join together to celebrate. Rodeos and county fairs, the biggest events of the year, even in growing places like Billings and Great Falls, bring out the population to show pride in who they are and their western heritage.

All six of the eastern third of the state's Indian Reservations have pow wows and other celebrations of their culture throughout the warm months. Events such as Crow Fair at Crow Agency, North American Indian Days at Browning and Red Bottom Days at Frazer are highlights of life in these native sovereignties.

To experience this very special piece of Montana, point your iron chariot, bike, horse or feet east of where the wall of mountains ends. Take the side roads, enter every town, travel slowly and grasp the powerful aura and vastness of this uncommon landscape.

Let the words and photos of this book provoke and entice your curiosity. You have to see it, only a first hand experience will make you a believer. Go often and in every season.

Rick Graetz
Matador Ranch, Little Rocky Mountains
Zortman, Montana
June 2000

Morning fog lifts from the Medicine Lake National Wildlife Refuge.
RICK AND SUSIE GRAETZ

The historic Matador
Ranch looking west
towards the Little
Rocky Mountains
south of Malta.
RICK AND SUSIE GRAETZ

Birdtail Butte
west of Cascade.
JOHN LAMBING

Snow Creek by Fort Peck Lake and the Charles M. Russell National Wildlife Refuge.
RICK AND SUSIE GRAETZ

Please don't eat the daisies. In the east foothills of the Wolf Mountains.
RICK AND SUSIE GRAETZ

A distinct region unto itself,

Montana east of the mountains harbors

unique landforms.

13

Sundown over the
Missouri River from
Round Butte north
of Jordan.
RICK AND SUSIE GRAETZ

The splendor of
spring. Ear Mountain
on the Rocky
Mountain Front.
JOHN LAMBING

16

 Old homestead
in the Missouri
Breaks north
of Roy.
RICK AND SUSIE GRAETZ

The first rays
of the sun
illuminate the
rims of the
Bighorn Canyon,
the Pryor
Mountains in
the distance.
RICK AND SUSIE GRAETZ

Fort Peck Lake from
Wagon Coulee south
of Glasgow.
RICK AND SUSIE GRAETZ

The Sweetgrass Hills
north of Shelby
and Chester.
RICK AND SUSIE GRAETZ

20

A storm trails
off above Sand
Creek on the
CMR National
Wildlife Refuge.
RICK AND SUSIE GRAETZ

This is a land of

great character.

Rampart like rims
form a backdrop
for the town of
Winnett.
RICK AND SUSIE GRAETZ

Near Bitter Creek,
northwest of
Glasgow.
RICK AND SUSIE GRAETZ

23

The view of Square
Butte near Geraldine
from the Bears Paw
Mountains.
RICK AND SUSIE GRAETZ

Prairie flowers
out perform a
summer storm.
DOUGLASS DYE

In winter, turbulent blizzards leave

comforters of snow in their wake.

The old bridge
over the Missouri
River out of
Wolf Point.
RICK AND SUSIE GRAETZ

Ice flow on the
Missouri River
north of Great Falls.
CHUCK HANEY

Strip farming
near Big Sandy
beneath the Bears
Paw Mountains.
JOHN LAMBING

28

In-between fire calls.
The daily cribbage
tournament at
Jordan.
RICK AND SUSIE GRAETZ

Missouri Breaks
badlands north of
Jordan.
RICK AND SUSIE GRAETZ

The Marias River
south of Chester.
CHUCK HANEY

34

Prairie pot
holes east of
Plentywood
and north of
Culbertson.
LARRY MAYER

Pompey's Pillar
and the Yellowstone
River.
LARRY MAYER

36

The Wild and
Scenic Missouri
River.
RICK AND SUSIE GRAETZ

A *playing field*

for clouds and weather.

Bowdoin National
Wildlife Refuge
out of Malta.
CHUCK HANEY

White Cliffs on
a segment of the
Wild and Scenic
Missouri River.
CHUCK HANEY

40

Evening quiet
west of Westby
on the Comertown
Preserve.
HAROLD E. MALDE

The Powder River
as it enters
Montana south
of Broadus.
RICK AND SUSIE GRAETZ

You have to see it, only

a first hand experience

will make you a believer.

Spring hits
the Big Snowy
foothills.
RICK AND SUSIE GRAETZ

The Wolf
Mountains on
the Bar V Ranch.
RICK AND SUSIE GRAETZ

44

Terry Badland's
magic light.
RICK AND SUSIE GRAETZ

Ready for harvest
south of Moore.
RICK AND SUSIE GRAETZ

46

Fort Benton
waterfront.

49

Spring storm
north of Shelby.
RICK AND SUSIE GRAETZ

Fort Peck Lake.
SALVATORE VASAPOLLI

On the road to
Snow Creek north
of Jordan.
RICK AND SUSIE GRAETZ

Northern Bighorn
Mountains on the
Crow Reservation.
RICK AND SUSIE GRAETZ

Take the side roads, travel slowly,

grasp the powerful aura

and vastness of this uncommon landscape.

52

Early morning
from a Marias
River canoe camp.
RICK AND SUSIE GRAETZ

The Big Muddy
Country north
of the Scobey —
Plentywood road.
RICK AND SUSIE GRAETZ

54

"Charlie Russell
Square Butte"
southwest of
Great Falls.
RICK AND SUSIE GRAETZ

The *Old West* of legend

was played here.

The Bear Paw Battlefield-Nez Perce National Monument south of Chinook.
RICK AND SUSIE GRAETZ

The Rocky Mountain Front near Kiowa and north of Browning on the Blackfeet Reservation.
RICK AND SUSIE GRAETZ

A thunderstorm
roars over the
Judith Mountains
near Lewistown.
LARRY MAYER

61

Lonesome prairie
north of Ingomar
and the Jersey
Lilly.
RICK AND SUSIE GRAETZ

A grain elevator
east of Shelby.
CHUCK HANEY

A formidable canopy of sky provides

a constantly changing panorama.

The Powder River
Country south of
Miles City.
RICK AND SUSIE GRAETZ

Watering the
wildflowers near
Wolf Point.
DOUGLASS DYE

64

The Yellowstone
River Valley
near Worden.
LARRY MAYER

Bull elk.
ERWIN AND PEGGY BAUER

Fog shrouds the
Billing's rimrocks.
LARRY MAYER

68

From Dupuyer
a sunrise lights
up the Sweetgrass
Hills far to the
northeast.
RICK AND SUSIE GRAETZ

The Beartooth
Mountains loom
behind the church
at Luther.
LARRY MAYER

The confluence
of the Yellowstone
and Missouri rivers
near Fairview and
Sidney.
CHUCK HANEY

Space, much of it undisturbed,

is its greatest commodity.

To the Native Americans

the children are sacred...

Young Crow Fair
participant.
RICK AND SUSIE GRAETZ

From the rim of the
Chalk Buttes
looking northeast
— near Ekalaka.
RICK AND SUSIE GRAETZ

74

Between
Columbus and
Red Lodge, near
Roscoe, the
mountains end
and the prairie
heads east.
RICK AND SUSIE GRAETZ

Makoshika Park
at Glendive.
RICK AND SUSIE GRAETZ

Rock Creek Canyon
north of Hinsdale.
RICK AND SUSIE GRAETZ

The Musselshell
River near
Ryegate.
RICK AND SUSIE GRAETZ

The Rock Creek
area northwest
of Glasgow.
RICK AND SUSIE GRAETZ

The *abundance of wildlife*

in this domain is legendary.

Bighorn sheep
on the CMR.
ERWIN AND PEGGY BAUER

Pedestal Rock in
the Tongue River
Breaks.
SALVATORE VASAPOLLI

Near the town
of Fort Shaw, the
Rocky Mountain
Front.
RICK AND SUSIE GRAETZ

From the top
of the Big Snowies
looking west towards
the Little Belts and
Judith Gap.
RICK AND SUSIE GRAETZ

A cannola
field changes
the color of the
landscape near
Valier.
RICK AND SUSIE GRAETZ

Bringing them home near Decker and the Tongue River Valley.
RICK AND SUSIE GRAETZ

Bighorn Canyon National Recreation Area and the east face of the Pryor Mountains.
RICK AND SUSIE GRAETZ

Cattle outfits here have been in the same family for generations.

88

The Pryor
Mountains south
of Billings.
RICK AND SUSIE GRAETZ

Clinker or scoria
surfaced road
north of Ekalaka.
RICK AND SUSIE GRAETZ

An agricultural
horizon west of
Glasgow.
RICK AND SUSIE GRAETZ

Reminders of the past

remain evident.

Bighorn Battlefield
National Monument
near Crow Agency.
RICK AND SUSIE GRAETZ

Looking north
from Eagle's Nest
Point east of Scobey.
RICK AND SUSIE GRAETZ

Above the
Missouri River
near Fort Benton
looking towards
the Highwood
Mountains.
RICK AND SUSIE GRAETZ

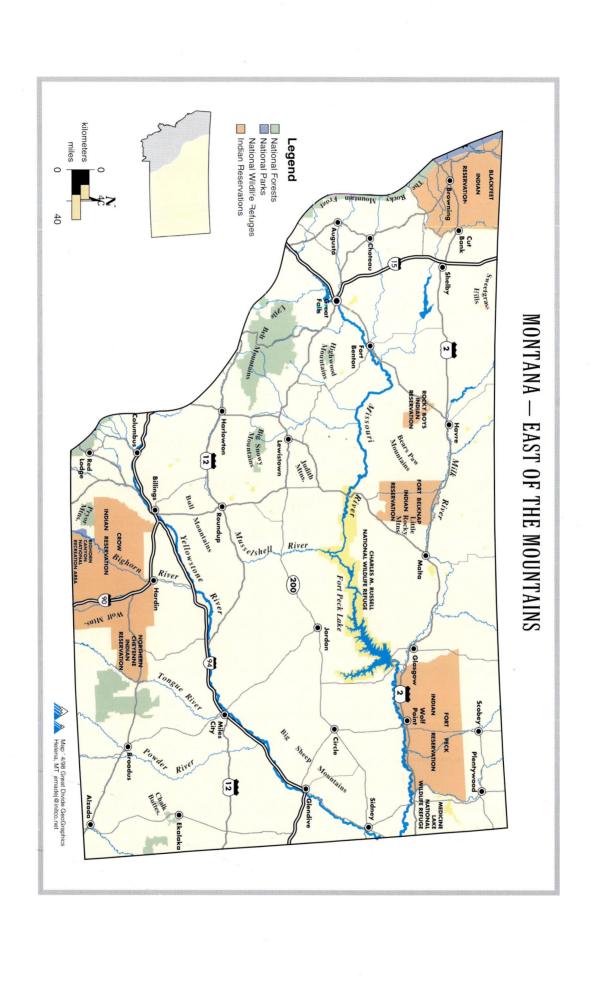

MONTANA — EAST OF THE MOUNTAINS

Legend
- Indian Reservations
- National Wildlife Refuges
- National Parks
- National Forests

kilometers
miles

0
0
40
40

N

BLACKFEET
INDIAN
RESERVATION

Browning
Cut Bank
Shelby
Sweetgrass Hills
The Rocky Mountain Front
Augusta
Choteau
Great Falls
Lake
15
2
Havre
ROCKY BOYS
INDIAN
RESERVATION
Bear's Paw Mountains
Missouri River
Fort Benton
Highwood Mountains
Belt Mountains
Judith Mtns.
FORT BELKNAP
INDIAN
RESERVATION
Little Rocky Mtns.
Malta
Harlowton
Lewistown
Big Snowy Mountains
12
CHARLES M. RUSSELL
NATIONAL WILDLIFE REFUGE
Fort Peck Lake
Glasgow
2
Wolf Point
FORT PECK
INDIAN
RESERVATION
Scobey
Plentywood
MEDICINE
LAKE
NATIONAL
WILDLIFE REFUGE
Columbus
Billings
Red Lodge
Pryor Mtns.
BIGHORN CANYON NATIONAL RECREATION AREA
CROW
INDIAN
RESERVATION
Bighorn
Hardin
Wolf Mtns.
NORTHERN CHEYENNE INDIAN RESERVATION
Bull Mountains
Roundup
Musselshell River
Yellowstone River
200
Jordan
Circle
Sidney
Glendive
12
Miles City
Big Sheep Mountains
94
Tongue River
Powder River
Broadus
Alzada
Chalk Buttes
Ekalaka